WHY THE WILL TO PUNISH?

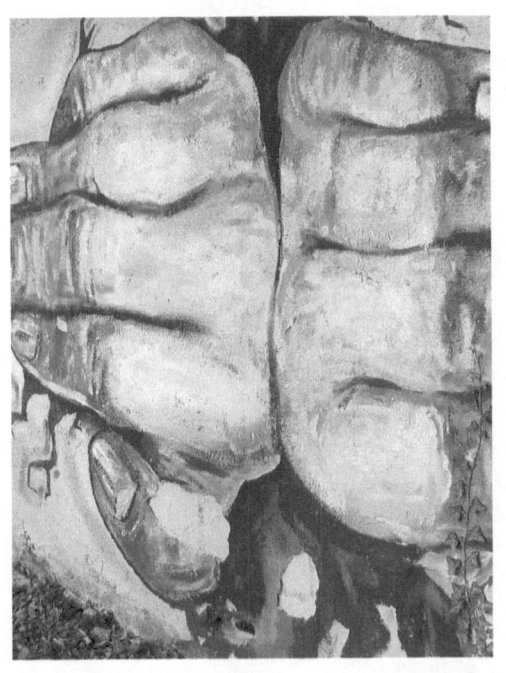

POEMS BY MICHAEL POAGE

Spartan
Press

Spartan Press

Kansas City, Missouri

spartanpresskc.com

 Spartan
Press

Copyright © Michael Poage, 2023

First Edition: 1 3 5 7 9 10 8 6 4 2

ISBN: 978-1-958182-46-8

LCCN:2023946941

Cover image: Jon Lee Grafton

Interior image: Martin Frljic, 2014, Mostar,

Bosnia and Herzegovina. Photo by author.

Author photos: Dr. Gretchen Eick

"Inhumation" first published in RHINO

Table of Contents

YOU FORGIVE, IN THEORY

THE WHOLE BRIGHT TOWN SIGHS

PHYSICAL EDUCATION

I AM USING SATIRE, OR NOT

To the disappeared

Before you heal someone, ask them if they are willing to give up the things that make them sick.

-Hippocrates

The poor may speak to you of emptiness, but he cannot give you his hunger.

The refugee may speak to you of leaving, but he cannot give you his downed.

-Threa Almontaser, *The Wild Fox of Yemen*

YOU FORGIVE, IN THEORY

THE FRONT LINE

Boulevar, Mostar, Bosnia and Herzegovina 2020

Today I met a lifetime goal.
I was walking behind an old man,
Perhaps five or ten years younger
Than me. We were practicing
Good social distancing because
Of the COVID-19 pandemic as if
Some paramilitary 20-year old
Had shouted us into the direction
Of a death camp. We were walking
Slowly because, this time, no one was
Rushing us along the Boulevar, the front
Line in the 1990's wars, new buildings
Shined in the sunlight like those advertisements
For vacations in Dubai. Then the tall
Bombed out Sniper's Tower standing watch
Over it all. I watched him as he so
Skillfully clasped his hands behind
His back as he walked, as he thought.
I realized that I had been waiting – not
Consciously – to get to that age where I
Could put my own hands together
Behind my back, lean a little forward,
Walk along the front line, dignified,
Wise, pondering the future or the past,
Wise and tired as a Bosnian old man.

SPACIAL PREPOSITIONS

Mostar, BiH siege, 1993 – 1994

What is beautiful
when there is
no world?

Do only fools
walk in
the cold?

The trumpet
is dead so why
are you moving?

Only the crows
come for a coffee,
and the sadly

Sad. Now they will
die to whom
they write

a sentence. Why
the will
to punish?

FERAL

--Front line, Mostar, 1993

I just found out that the brain
Uses up calories. You all knew
That, right, having paid attention
In biology class? I knew some things
And enjoyed the dissection of
The frog more than most. But I am
Now distracted by the lace curtains
In my study and the feral pink sky

As the sun sets, as usual, in the west.
I lose track of my job, at this window,
Here on the front line, the boulevard
Below, as a sniper looking for movement.
I am a lousy soldier and pay
For it. They called it a flesh wound.

SOAP

Sometimes it's the ancient
ordinary things that
gets the stink blowed
off you. If it's a lively
breeze then you hope it is
from the north. It's the best
for scouring words like that one
from the skin with some guarantee
of a day or two clean. But
when you go to the south wind,
the Slavic twist from Blagai
to your town, it brings the dust
and plastic bags flittering
like bats and then you glow
like the desert in the late sun
and face more need for sorcery
instead of scoury words. And
in the event of an unusual crosswind
bounding off the rocks of the mountains
surrounding your city, you are going
to be forced back to the ancient remedy.

THE MEDIUM HOTEL

A normal human life is all
you want. You can't find
it here in the midst of
family and lost books
you never wanted to read
anyway. You light another
cigarette, your fifth in
six minutes. You claim
you have lost seven years
of your life. You tell me
you are religious so why
has all this happened, you ask?

Anyplace but here will help.
No more medium, screwed up
people in your life. You
will find another hotel where
they appreciate your work, –
leaving good tips, no gentle
words of thanks, and no one
falls in love with you.

MARE ON MY CHEST

I don't know sometimes where
to find the hope when friends
die and nephews take themselves
out. Anger is just another
loss. The clouds wish they
could dump all that rain
and move on. The earth is
desperate for rescue although
the chances are as good as in
Vegas. The skin I imagine
is just that. Outside, along
the Neretva some dog, a new one,
barks and sets off some car
alarm we should all pay attention to.
Anger is just another loss.

NOTE FOUND IN THE NERETVA

just like my frig
but I don't have
any magnets
from America
you will have to send
me a package
but with magnets and
all kinds of magic things
and some postcards in it
and so much love
just arrived home
from work
how are you

INHUMATION

The hardest part
is breaking the ground.

This is not the bog
of peat that would

preserve the human
into sometimes even

clearer recognition. This
is hard pan breaking

the shovels forcing us
to curse the ground

but even then it is
nothing but the lazy

lace of bones anywhere
they might land

and the scattering of
shoes, underwear, of family

resemblance, leaving only
a wide space for the jaw.

AGITA

You are Italian-Bosnian
with anxiety and stress –
normal – but how do you
tell me what you are feeling?
What do you care about most now?

Our life is like a bone on bone
knee, no mediating cartilage to
stop the scraping, save our love.

PERILS OF POMEGRANITES

The bone chill of morning concentration
brings a quiet across the meadow Bosniak
broken by the last of the underage girls raped
by daddy generals as upstanding citizens of our
beautiful city and the mountains beyond. If you
have the stomach to read a few lines of allegations
or witness testimony which ice the blood, read on, and on

BOSNIAN CATENATIVE VERBS

Thousands of miles, face to face
During that day
In the museum in Travnik
You taste the
Bitter air, the lips of so much striving,
The tongue struggling to make
A grammar of love like the paintings
Of Monet, one lily pond hundreds
Of times, close enough
For an illegal touch. The ambiguous gossip
Of color with verbs brushed
Into each other like our love
Was an accident of one
Infinitive after another, infinite
Across an ocean with syntax
Like 'I love that man,' poetic
Catenatives that live thousands
Of miles, face to face.

BAILIWICK

Above a whisper
or below a whisper
what will you find?
A place of safety
or one of fear?

Don't ask me so many
questions, am I the one
under suspicion?

You may go but be
warned that the raven
is watching you. You
could be sent back
to the old country
anytime. I watch
the birds carefully,
all kinds of birds,
not because I am afraid

but the opposite.
The wings and the
flight give me hope.
What about you
tasting that orange,

do you know how
mean we can all be
above or below
that Balkan whisper?

the whole bright town sighs

BEYOND THAT

He wore his time
on his wrist, a circle
of blue. Beyond that
his hope
for a lasting
kindness born
of the toughness
of life. He learned
about being kind
when he felt
on his own skin
the lack of it.

SUPERHERO

across the sky and late adolescence
the last trick from the bag
is lost, somewhere you misplaced it
and you are in front of everyone. they
watch your dark eyes as if you
are the horror show. you could scare
all of them to death if you felt the
power over them they know you
have. but these perverse hormones
only frighten you, leave you standing
naked. there is no strength of will
as you hope for a superhero to swoop
down and save you from the laughter
and take you away from all that is
peripheral, emulated, or cross-legged.

COGNITIVE FLEXIBILITY

In theory, you dream a dragon
Spreading its wings with the anxiety
Of anyone trying to avoid St. George
Or another, front-of-the-cave,
Near-death, experience.

Wave upon wave to crush
The bones of daily beasts and reality-
Based plot lines trolling the waters
Of the loch where the mist hangs
Right over the stain of the disappeared.

It has grown to be an epidemic
As we all look over our shoulders
While others watch ahead, alert to find us
To keep us quiet forever. It is almost a matter
Of faith, of careful breathing, as we fall.

Infinity is a natural wonder, more egregious
And circumspect than any flight of birds
Making its way to a southern continent now
Drifting alone in a lonely sea where it can only
Be discovered like Neptune, by numerical prediction.

You dream again about the dragon
But now you are the one spreading your wings
Tough as an ancient angel. Your voice makes
Silent the meadows and mountains pounding the
Earth for mercy. It is finished, you forgive, in theory.

DIVINE COMEDY

You have
a sense of humor
like the ornate
box turtle
our state
reptile. But,
I am told,
it's all in
the timing.
So,
I wait.

AGORAPHOBIA

You just want to close your eyes to the world.
Instead, you'll just stay within the walls,
prison-like, of this house. And smoke. And drink
coffee. The neighbor will bring the mail and paper
to your door. What happened in your childhood
to make you cringe at the thought of shopping, going
out to dinner with friends? You watch morning
T.V., the afternoon soaps for some drama. And
the news. The news. That's it. You glance outside.

REFUGEE

My whole system is geared
For the good old days, hour
After hour of removing life
Support while the faithful
Wife organizes grief sessions
For the kids and embracing
The doctor and nurses, thanking
Them for all we have done,
Says we feel like family
And please stay in touch
For old times sake. A few
Drinks later she will
Volunteer for the inner circle
Of an Italian drama based
On Dante. She will flesh out
All the unfortunate refugees
Making it this far but having
Everything against them, they
Stumbled back into the sea.

The Theremin

you waited until they died
then you officially buried them
all. why? you had some
secret grudge against wailing?
you didn't like early electric
music? just caress the air with
your hands and you have music,
eerie, something very strange but
delicious. maybe the metal antennas
reminded you of some childhood
incident. but you did not get
them all, sorry to tell you.
official or not, some escaped
and are waiting for your visit.
wave your hands your delicate way,
let the theremin weep and wail.

THE WEATHER (forecast/foreplay)

I am barely a woman at all.
Have you seen how small I am?
Of course not, never in all these
layers of pink, brown and red.
Not to mention this large umbrella
that would cover my entire naked
body. I bought it because of
the weather forecast I saw this
morning. I turned it on as I
was dressing to come here. The woman
had bare arms, a tan and was good
at forecasting. I tried to imitate her
movements, the way she seemed to
caress the magic map even though
I know she did not actually come near
touching even one of those countries.
But I liked her tactics, wanted to feel
the touch I wanted to feel in my life.
And you can be sure, as I tap your knee
when we talk that I am playing with the weather
forecast, with you, with us as you watch me slowly
twirl this new umbrella I bought today because
of the forecasting lady. Maybe, it will rain
and I will need to decide whether or not
to share this new, large umbrella with you.

FAKE SKELETON WITH HAT

It was worth a try.
Maybe he was constantly
Late for work. Or perhaps
He was a practitioner
Of comedy, or, given his
Passenger, tragedy. He is one
Of 7,000 a year who illegally
Use the HOV lane in Arizona.

He was spotted by the authorities
Who saw the strange companion.
First, the hat, then the skull
Under the hat. The offender was
Only wanting to be in the fast lane,
Only wanting to be on time, finally.

THE CROFTER

It's the muddling around
in the croft with the blue and blighted door
that gives you the reputation
up one street, down another
until it crawls and sweeps with its long
flesh-punched tail finally
back into the secret lake
and the whole bright town sighs its globed relief.

RUN FACING TRAFFIC

Time to go,
I can just
sense it.
Not fear,
as I realized
today. Because
I have survived.
Carefully, look
straight into the
headlights, carry
the burden
of your race,
the foot steps
behind you,
the hard breathing
but even, like the
stride, a healthy
heart, the movement
of air, never give anyone
a free shot, always,
always run facing the traffic.

PENCIL

Coloring the page
I am told to stay
Within the lines,
This color or
That one for the
Eyes or the tail.

But the creature on
The page before
My eyes is wanting
A color of its own.
Cries out for
A sharp pencil.

To grasp in it's fist to
Tear through the paper
One corner to the
Other, across the
Page, creating a
Crumbled, forbidden life.

A FLIGHT TO SOMEWHERE

I have forgotten those times
others call memorable. My
most intimate mysteries,
simply not knowing when to stop --
lovely, slight, hurtful
and up to my waste
in the swirling sea looking like
a calendar photo. I simply
didn't know when to stop.

"Go t' sleep ya' little baby"

It's as simple a beginning as this
and as difficult. What will come next?
A walk along the sea two hundred miles
from Norway? The glowing green night sky
stuns your nerves, a lucid reminder
of the little we know as the bedtime
rituals with our children bring our sea-bones
aching up to the surface, are carried by
the tides towards the islands as a gift
wrapped in salt, faltering with each step.
Please, all ye babies, the harp blesses your sleep.

EARTHQUAKES IN KANSAS

Here are my mom and dad on a good day:
That was before the earthquakes began
And they stopped standing for photographs,
Stopped standing near each other. They each
Had their individual press conferences with
Rage and erotic dimensions but mostly
Martial law, clever, self-assured until
She left and he drove off the road on a
Dark turn, the red car filled with ecstasy,
His body flying from Tecate toward Yuma.

GAZA SONNET #1

Having bombed the children,
homes, hospitals,
used phosphorus
on the playgrounds
pieces bouncing onto
the skin of six-year old's
it burns and keeps
burning its way *(scream here!)*

through to the bone.
It's a long way to the sea.
It's a long way to the sea.
It's a long way to the sea.
It's a long way to the sea.
It's a long way, my children.

WHEAT

Here are some of those things:
Gradually the system begins
to break down with ransom
and capture. Soon the snow, as we
will see, never measures up to
expectations. Here in south central,
the meadowlark sits on the remaining
brick foundation bringing her particular
ballad to Vermont Street. And the wheat
being in the ground, red winter
can begin. It took four days after removing
life support. Red winter has begun.

Physical Education

LETTER

Hi, I am fine, thanks
for asking. For the first
time I had therapy
two days in a row. It was
helpful but also brought
up a lot of crap
and questions. I believe
I was sexually abused
by my 5th grade teacher
during a summer when he
brought me and another male
classmate to his summer
cottage at Cape Cod. I can't
remember specifics,
hardly any details
but my gut passes on
secret information to me.

The week at the Cape
was supposed to be an honor
as only two boys were selected –
each summer. Anyway, today
I am not doing so great,
with the leftover taste of
salt water in my mouth.

GARDEN

If it blooms
it's a flower.
You never weed
the garden
because it is all
unknown and
beautiful. Besides,
what have those
wild plants
done to you?

MOTHER, MAY I?

You tell everyone you are well
but not about
the hauntings. You notice
the relief on their faces
that they have asked you
as promised, not
that you are well.
That you are well
is not of concern,
not, as promised. Why do
they say the light is blinding?
The "suspicious" brushfire in L.A.
is growing. The morgue at al Shifa
is filled with strips of anonymous flesh
and splintered bones of the children.
You tell everyone you are well
but not about
the hauntings you notice.

IRIS

There is a message
in that word.
For real. And you
can discover the

truth by caution
and straight talk
before the marriage,
look – the purple and white.

TANGLE EYE

We all keep
Working on what
It means
To be human.
That is the summary.
Some win prizes,
Get interviews on NPR.
You have kept looking
Straight ahead
All your life
With one eye
Staring at the sun,
The other tangled
In hope
For what it means.

2 POEMS IN BODY OF EMAIL

The flesh plucked roughly away
Told the father and son finding
The two poems in the shallows
That the body had been dead

For some time. No identification
Found with either of them and no
Family to make final arrangements.
The sacred words came from a stranger.

A HISTORY OF OKLAHOMA

We have the best
documented life with you
having been conceived
in the Upper Volta
or maybe the southern flow
of the Neosho. It's a
matter of record no one
wrote down. Fortunate
for you no photographs
remain. Memory tells you there is only
last year, then Jesus,
the Renaissance, then
of course, you are limited
in your rage to dirt roads,
one continent
and a father exploring
the unknown, previously
taught as flat,
world.

PONY, MONTANA

1.

The bridge, made of large concrete squares, held
    for the moment.

2.

She told me there was suffocation in the room.

3.

It is all one-sided, you always pouring yourself into
    the cup.

4.

She laid on the floor for two days, her right leg
    paralyzed, saying, "It's not mine."

5.

In Spanish, if a negative follows a verb, a negative
    must precede the verb, it's the rule.

6.

There is that urge again, to run away to open ground.

7.

She said that the sky was raining but only horse tears.

8.

The Girl Scouts' pumpkin carving is still on.

9.

In kindergarten I was the one in show & tell with a
time limit.

10.

Dismal seems like a brighter word than desolation.

BLIND OUTLET

No one wants to be around anymore.
I just don't have any vivid memories
recognizing a halt or sublime
performance some idea like the
invasion of the beauty spring in the languaging
of the mouth and languishing
when we can. Circe is popular now
and may be around the corner, around
the bed, hanging out. She might
want to be with you with her own visiting
memories. Welcome traveler. My promise
if you sleep with me is survival
and a permanent shadow.

PHOTO FROM SCOTLAND #2

Today
the sea   is full

of white horses. Far out the blue
is calm
like the music
of the harp

with breath   in and breath   out.
Simple. And is my
rage the same? I talk to some friend
or stranger then the   familiar
desire

comes
to him or to her
in the face with my already
automatically
clenched fist and/but I make love

to the white horses
full of the sea.

DUBLIN AIRPORT

Magdalena is called for her flight
to Brussels. We all follow her
onto the bus taking us to the connecting
plane. It is an ecstatic time for everyone.
The temperature has dropped to 7 Celsius.
Celtic is in the air as a Jet Blue plane
takes off into the dark morning sky.
Jesus, she says to me. I say, don't touch
me, yet. We'll all meet later – in Brussels –
Magdalena, me, the disciples. Then Judas
whispered in my ear to save embarrassment.
Sir, this is not your flight. You have been
enchanted by a false heart. Remember, stay
away from love, then you won't risk betrayal.

AVINE FUNERAL

it's a variant form
of avian to be used
in mortified ways
to change the living
wing-work of the flames
of birds all around
this house and the sea,
variant love-making
the darkness dash against
the last trees left
in this lush landscape
and from Heaven escape
to invert evil to live
dashing night to diamonds.

THE RIGHT TO BE FORGOTTEN: A SONNET

The sea birds are a morning chorus,
restive in their wakefulness. Soon
the same lonely coastal music
will bring the restless
waves to the point of breaking and invoke
the "right to be forgotten."
In these countries, under the force
of legal power you or someone you love

can be forgotten, it is the legal
right to be deleted. So often there have been
those times when you have wanted
to just disappear, never to be seen again
or remembered like so many soldiers or children
invading an unknown beach, dragged out to sea.

SOUTHWEST FL. 36

Ok, babe,
we need you,
Paul Wright,
if you're still
going to Little Rock
we are here, babe,
Gate 20, the door
is still open.
Or, babe, listen,
you could join some
of these soldiers
and go to Ft. Campbell
although you might need
basic, training I mean,
you could go to Syria
with the elites, babe,
figure it out, I'm
closing the door, honey,
I need you.

EIGHTH GRADE

I was the kid who hid
in the arts
and crafts closet
in eighth grade. It was
fear. It was dance time
for Physical Education
which terrified me.
Dancing and being educated
physically.

MAYBE A RIB

It was funeral food.
Everyone sat at round
tables, heads down as
they chewed and swallowed,
swallowed and coughed.
Eight people could sit
at each table though
each table was overflowing.

I watched as people moved
their lips as if talking
to the next person. No sound
collided with any other
sound to create completed
words. Eyes were barely
open like the tears, barely.

The young girls chose the wrong
house for a sleep over. Rage
was the language choking
on the tongue. It was
funeral food. A few guests
went back for seconds, more
lime jello, coffee, or a rib.

THE TREE

A skinny tree comes into view
Plodding along on a very distant
Handmade pathway. Too much
Of that world is in this world.
I imagine everyone wearing two
Sets of clothes, pajamas for sleep
And the work clothes worn over them
Since there is only sleep and work,
Sleep and work. Today I read
A poem by Nye where she uses
"even-ing," and the "resonance of moor"
On the Isle of Mull, Scotland.
Because we worry about friends
Back on the North Sea coast of
Scotland, it matters, all that salt
Tide and the dark-ing of rock.

ELISIONS

The light is in the center
of the ceiling. You will return
because soon friends will be dying
and you will be asked
to officiate the funeral
or visit them in their sickness,
say comforting words, try
to get them to smile.
It will be an act of breaking away
or of joining together, something,
in either case, of eternal omission.

THE CORRUPTION OF ADVENT

O, how shall I receive thee
Rend the heavens wild
Light the lamp of the Baptists cry?
Soon we'll all be near ye.

Bring the gifts of gold and myrrh
Twisted star, broken heart
Expect the father's child to leap
Soon to birth the angel's word.

FRESH FISH SOLD HERE #1

It's an old joke
like fumbleheed
but I can't remember it
so
I should ask
the person who told me.

Go down, go down.
I can't find
the person
with information
about this old joke
because she is in the states
and I am in Bosnia
and Herzegovina,
perhaps you know?

Or
maybe Faulkner
could devise a machine
to find gold
and jokes or some other
mystery in the cotton
lynching and here we start

to get serious. You can't run,
you can't jog, get out of a car

without risking your life
to the fumbleheed, not
a joke. Go down, Moses.
Go down, *mmmmmm*

mazing.

IMPEDIMENT

His head hurts
thinking about having
to put words
in his mouth.
So much the enemy.

The snatching away
of syllables by electrified
muscle tissue
shoots of pain rooting
everywhere from brain

to legs. He has to think
about every phoneme
hours ahead of time. He needs
some space, not someone
jumping in to "help"

which it doesn't. He gets angry
when you can't just wait
for his inside sparks
to catch up to the larynx
tongue. And then the blood

on the tongue, the repetition
of sound, the same damn
sound. Always the same sound

as something cramming words
up his throat

against the will.
So much the enemy.
Against the brain and pediment
into sharp pain blood
pooling around the white teeth.

AN OLDER MAN

Fifty years later, following some death,
I arranged for the fate
of my next fire. I consciously oppressed
my soul's cousin
and was told I could now only sing solo.

I AM USING SATIRE, OR NOT

GLEMM BULK FOOD GOSPEL
BOOKSTORE

Does this mean the food
Is bulky, awkward to handle,
Impossible to grip with two hands or four
Or you can buy it by the case
Or pallet-load to put in the back
Of the truck until three months
Is up and you return
To stock up on provisions?
Unlike a monograph this writing
Is on multiple subjects like horses,
Windows, empty stomachs, bad news,
Good news, land of the lost, land of the
Brave, cowardice, open doors, rain,
Ice, books, food, no food, water, no
Water, music, cacophony, green,
Soil, seeds, frustration,
Defeat, victory, frustration (again), buttress,
Voice, no voice, rage, laughter, hope
Humor. Preach this list then comeback
To me. I will load your pickup, don't bother
About the tip you never bothered with
In the first place. Vocabulary cards will help
Your total education. It will help you hold
Your fist high in the air, o my children,
Give away the bulk food, the books, the good
News as is only fair and true, bulky with hope.

INFLECTION POINT

A frog on my window
Is swept off
By the windshield wiper.
I drive down the street
In the humidity of
This tropical brain fog.

The war is long over
But my lungs
I gave to the blue
Soldier near the river
Crawling toward me
Pleading for a deep breath.

We are all having
Strange and violent nightmares
Since August. It has been
Documented. Suicides? Yes.
Domestic violence? Yes.
The blood streaks across the windshield.

TOWARD THE BITTER LAKES

The water is kind to me today
carrying me as if affectionate
to a new edge of the wild.

In the foreseeable future which
is returning in the old naïve
way as if affectionate to the edge.

With the intuition of a stroke or an
earthquake, she took my hand as if
with kind intention leading me to the lake.

conditional logic

low pressure moving
across the region
is expected

so I am wary
of you risking
it all. you say his way
of thinking is
fascinating,
so is covid-19, the spikes

to bring an unsettled day.

a swarm of bees

for George Floyd

it's only a video sent
by a friend. her father's
bees embracing a branch
and the trunk of a tree
moving barely enough
to notice. in fact, the first
thing is the sound. a
grinding, slow business
cooking above your head,
without hurry, no place
to go without your mama,
so the charge is stinging
without intent to kill.

Introducing

on behalf of the others,
those who couldn't be,
for whatever reason
just couldn't,
be. But in their absence
let me acknowledge
the courage of the saints
not with us, the holiest
of fathers who will never
say their goodbye's not
because they are dead
but from simple lying
completely to the end.
May they return in peace
to face the sons and daughters,
to face the children who have
truly died right before their eyes.

POPE CANCELS EASTER FOR PUBLIC

Easter, 2020

This is Italy, spring, 2020.
It's hard to explain to you
exactly what fear! I'm being
wrapped up in a cocoon of anther
from the flame or the flower
burning as we speak of deep
yearning for touch and freedom,
hands waving in the air, the gloss
in the sky with a dangerous
proximity. With Easter canceled
for the public, we are on our own
to find some loose hope floating,
just buoyant in the air. Since we
are the public we should unify
and find the Easter evidently

taking place even though not for
us. We can be creative. We can
be alert. When you discover some
light, stumble across options
in some field, let the rest of us know.
Shout it out. Hope cannot be canceled
even for the least of these, or the last.

SEVENTH SYMPHONY

Can you hear the flute
Maybe in the last movement
Like heaven although better
Because I don't know what
Heaven is like, not really,
Not at all. But I can hear
And see the flute in Leningrad,
The city of Lenin. Slavic. Frozen
In the siege. Then the strings dance
For the dead wrapped in sheets
Lying on sleds to be taken away.
The muted trumpets carry
Their tune across the mountain
West, the great desert, more
Mountains and then the sea
To shatter the glass towers
Built for other tragedies
And heroes. A friend asked,
Do they serve bourbon in
Heaven? Again, I know nothing
About heaven. Why, all at once,
Are people asking me about religion?
And why, all of a sudden, are TV news
Reporters showing so much anger
Toward elected officials and saying
To their colleagues, please stay safe, I love you?

PASSION FRUIT

The sky breaks open
on this Palm
Sunday-Passion Sunday-
the passion of my work
from the tree like fruit
too ripe for the hungers
of this world. But here
come the children
allowed their moment
of entry, carrying the palms
singing joyful "Alleluias"
for Jesus in greeting and
hopeful smiles. Forgive them
for they don´t know. Forgive
them for they don´t know
what is next. They cannot
hear the others singing,
"Hosanna," save us.

EASTER

Grief is familiar with all of us,
So full of possession and a sense
Of global warning. To be ravished
By the already cursed brings a
Medieval tone to this life and
So we watch the fortress gates
Carefully. No one in, no one out.
Carefully, the firing of the twenty-
One gun salute echoes west along
The rocks of the Scottish coast
Toward the Highlands where some
People have escaped for centuries
But usually not successfully. Hear
The philosophical lecture on the attempts
To escape from danger to hoped for
Safety. It is only philosophical and
The lecture ends early like a movie
Fade away into the dark. Remember,
With me you can never know
If I am using satire, or not.

WILDERNESS

The Snake River
into the Tetons
feeding this lake
big and cold,
I am told,
like your heart.

A MOMENT IN TIME

I wish someone
had a photograph.
Any photograph.
It is still a mystery
to me just how a
moment in time
and space can be
captured and made
to be still. Can
someone, anyone, help
me figure this out?
It doesn't feel right --
like Margaret Hayes
taking her last breath
right in front of me.

SHE DOESN'T LIKE WATER

You can cut all the flowers but you can't keep spring from coming.

-Neruda

Anything to drink but water. She hates it.
Maybe something from childhood
or a lost full moon or one of her children
strayed into traffic. But she only shows
strength and resilience in the worst of days
and nights of which she is so familiar. She would
even ask why people will ask if this poem is about
me. Do all poets really write about themselves?
Why can't this one be written in the third
person and mean it? People really do have
deep issues from childhood basements or
elementary teachers and their summer cottages.
She never could remember a wife being around. Soon
we all stray into the traffic and that word can
have many meanings like in the movie where
traffic means drugs, death, sadness, and ends
with a kid's baseball game on a dirt field
in Tijuana. Who forced her to drink water
when it was only pain for her? Does this poet
really mean water when that word is used? What
happened to her childhood? My bet is on the lost full moon.

re-forestation with stutter

watch the ferns in their
dense forni-
cation. don't be squeamish
like your br-
other or watch
too closely as
i did. father will be him-
self and push you ah-
way when you come
up to him
to say, I-
'm sorry.

ANCIENT TEXT (1)

A fragment

Gilgamish woke-up calling
For his mother in the midst
Of lusty dreams and omens.
"Mom! Like a Hittite of heaven
He fell on me, too heavy
For me." He had fear down around
His ankles, and felt a solitary
Childhood with ragged edges
And dogs betraying even their
Owners in the middle of the streets
And they all became his likeness.
Then "I loved him like a woman,"
Which is where the mother of
Gilgamish really started listening.

THE COMPLETE POEMS OF DEBBIE OCEAN

It is now the calm after the storm.

I want another word for hope, another language.

Are you in the mood for ultimate Karaoke?

Right now I have more children than problems.

Even full rhyme, like crime, doesn't pay.

I have a friend dying tonight in Bethlehem.

What 15th century Italian tried to make you American?

Put people with dogs in Room 407.

There's been another death in the community.

Beauty hurts, but do you know that much about pain?

You lived for two years in a tool shed.

Foot-washing on Maundy Thursday, not my thing.

How much healing can a person take?

I have an appointment with Mohammed at 10 this morning.

Dry air is the singer's enemy, but not the only one.

Michael Poage was born in Virginia. He has an MFA
in Creative Writing from the University of Montana and
an MDiv from San Francisco Theological Seminary.
This collection, WHY THE WILL TO PUNISH?, is
his fifteenth book of poetry. He served as the Poet-in-
Residence at Dzemal Bijedic University in Mostar, Bosnia
& Herzegovina, 2017-18 and received a Fellowship to
virtually teach English language and literature at Walailak
University in southern Thailand, 2021-22. He lives in
Wichita, Kansas with his wife, Dr. Gretchen C. Eick.

This project was made possible, in part, by generous
support from the Osage Arts Community.

Osage Arts Community provides temporary time, space
and support for the creation of new artistic works in a
retreat format, serving creative people of all kinds —
visual artists, composers, poets, fiction and nonfiction
writers. Located on a 152-acre farm in an isolated rural
mountainside setting in Central Missouri and bordered
by ¾ of a mile of the Gasconade River, OAC provides
residencies to those working alone, as well as welcoming
collaborative teams, offering living space and workspace
in a country environment to emerging and mid-career
artists. For more information, visit us at www.osageac.org

Osage Arts Community

www.ingramcontent.com/pod-product-compliance
Lightning Source LLC
Chambersburg PA
CBHW031446120626
46545CB00006B/2567